An Overthinker's Journal

A collection of poems

Ishita Bagchi

Ukiyoto Publishing

All global publishing rights are held by

Ukiyoto Publishing

Published in 2022

Content Copyright © Ishita Bagchi

ISBN 9789364948364

All rights reserved.
No part of this publication may be reproduced, transmitted, or stored in a retrieval system, in any form by any means, electronic, mechanical, photocopying, recording or otherwise, without the prior permission of the publisher.

The moral rights of the author have been asserted.

This is a work of fiction. Names, characters, businesses, places, events, locales, and incidents are either the products of the author's imagination or used in a fictitious manner. Any resemblance to actual persons, living or dead, or actual events is purely coincidental.

This book is sold subject to the condition that it shall not by way of trade or otherwise, be lent, resold, hired out or otherwise circulated, without the publisher's prior consent, in any form of binding or cover other than that in which it is published.

www.ukiyoto.com

Contents

It is never enough	1
Breaking patterns	2
Mirror image	4
Too much	5
Loving myself-one day at a time	6
When nostalgia hits	7
Searching for home	8
Disclaimer	9
A writer's den	10
Not a poem	11
Writing about heartbreak	12
To Calcutta, With Love	13
A receipe book on life	15
A letter to myself	16
In love with the nights	17
Love song	18
Facing my demons	20
My mind is a battlefield	21
Girls like us	22
Of appearances and love	23
Of dreams and fairylands	24
Nightmares	25
Paradoxes	26
Firsts	27
Building blocks	28
Stay	29
Parallel universe	30
Home	31

Someone like you	32
Indomitable	33
Opposites	34
Down the memory lane	36
Train of thoughts	38
Everytime	39
You & I	41
Bottled up	42
Beauty?	43
Not your cup of tea	44
Invincible	46
Our first date	47
One last time	48
Lights out	49
Departures	50
Seasons	51
Writers and their magic	52
Ruins	53
Missing	54
Forever?	55
Love in the times of pandemic	56
Confessions	57
About the Author	*58*

It is never enough

It is never enough for people who don't want to love you.
Your love, care, and affection are never enough for people who want to bypass you
when they are done with fulfilling their needs.
You will keep pouring into their cups,
draining yourself to the last drop
but their cup will still never be full.
You will do all that you can in your capacity to be their number one cheerleader,
their top priority,
and their go-to person.
But probably you will never be good enough for them to start with.

And you know why?
Because all this while you have only been putting the wrong people before yourself.
All this while you were only trying to keep a dead relationship alive that was never yours, to begin with, in the first place.
All this while you gave yourself away way more than you received.
What a fool you are! Isn't it?
Loving them,
breaking yourself apart a thousand times,
and still not giving up.

Breaking patterns

Remember when you met me for the first time?
You were a wreck and I was the anchor that you thought you needed.
You used to tell me that you wanted to write letters to me to express how you feel,
But you couldn't because you had spilt too much for someone else before
And now you don't know what to do with your empty heart.
You didn't know what to write or what to feel.
And I took your empty pages to fill them with what I wanted to write about you.
I took your empty heart to fill it with all the love I wanted to pour out to you.
Oh boy! I had so much to say to you.
Remember when you last walked out of my life saying that your lover had taken you back again and now you no longer need me as your lifeboat.
You found your home again and I, on the other hand, became homeless.
After you left, I didn't realise when I started to become your reflection.
Broken. Empty and emotionally a wreck.
You might be wondering why after almost 2 years, 3 months, and 18 days, I am suddenly writing to you.
Because today I met the older version of me in him.
Today when I met him, I saw his eyes full of innocence and a heart full of love exactly like they show in the sappy rom coms.
And he reminded me of all the things that you weren't and he is.
He reminded me of all that I wanted you to say to me but you never did.
He reminded me of all the times I tried hard to unravel your pain and heal you,
But you kept pushing me away.

And you know what else he reminded me of?
He reminded me of how I had to break the pattern of letting people walk all over me.
He showed me how important it is to take the leap of faith.
And that's why I decided to write this to you to say that I will not let another person's innocence and faith in love erode away which you so easily did to me.
I won't become the monster you were.
And I, I decided that I won't be you.

Mirror image

My mother is someone who can give warmth even to the coldest of hearts with her love.
My mother is someone who has always chosen tenderness over tough love.
They'd say that daughters are a mirror of their mothers.
And I,
I make a perfectly imperfect mirror of my mother.
A mirror that's far from being equivalent to a perfect daughter.
A mirror that's broken from the edges.
A mirror that has her heart jaded,
unlike her mother.
A mirror that has failed to reflect her mother's soul in a way the world wanted.
I'd always ask her,
"Mother, how can I become like you? How can I be your perfect reflection?"
She'd always laugh it away until one day when she told me,
"By being the exact version of yourself that you want to be."

Too much

People like us do not love in halves.
People like us are the ones whom they have labelled as "too much."
Too loud.
Too smart.
Too talkative.
Too mad.
Too crazy.
Too emotional.
People like us are the ones who are too much for them to deal with.
Because people like us overshare.
And overspill.
And maybe that's why the ones like us,
the ones who are "too much,"
become the misfits in the world of "too normal."
And maybe that's why people like us keep breaking piece by piece,
every time someone gets intimidated by us
and runs away abandoning us like an old dilapidated house.
People like us don't know what it means to maintain the mysterious aura around us
and how to play mind games
or adhere to the rule of law when it comes to expressing what we feel.
When people like us, who are "too much" love someone,
be it friends, lovers, or family,
love with all that they have because they don't know what loving with conditions means.
They don't know where to draw the boundary with their love
so that it doesn't break them apart.
After all, people like us do not love in halves.

Loving myself-one day at a time

I love how the curls of my hair quietly settle on my shoulders,
bearing the weight of my compulsive thoughts like a boulder.
I am in awe of my smile that is as bright as the summer sun,
 radiating happiness and fun.
When I stand in front of the mirror staring at my bare body
And naked soul,
My scars remind me of the pain that I have overcome.
My curves and creases narrate stories of the days when I skipped my exercise regime
And gorged on dessert to let go of my sadness.
Ironically, those were the days that made me hate myself a little less.
The cellulite on my stomach,
The stretch marks on my thighs were something that they thought would make me feel ashamed.
However, I wasn't the one to be tamed.
With each passing day, I started to embrace my body a little more.
And started loving myself to the core.
But don't get me wrong,
I wasn't the one who was madly in love with every nook and corner of my body.
I wasn't the one who always appreciated her curly hair,
her skin that is not so fair,
Or her broken teeth that always shone when she smiled.
It took me months or rather years
To overcome my fears
And pick myself up without shedding any tears.

When nostalgia hits

Years later,
on a random Sunday afternoon,
when you are cooking your favourite meal,
and you hear "Phir Le Aaya Dil" playing in the background,
old memories will hit you like a train.
You will recall the times when you had no clue
about how your dreams would take shape for you.
You will recall the times when you were heartbroken for the first time
and didn't know whether you would ever find love again.
And at that moment,
when you will look around you
and inhale the smell of your favourite freshly baked rum cookies,
you will realise that your clueless days and your crying sessions were all worth it.
You will know that what wasn't meant for you never stayed,
be it jobs, friends, or lovers.
And you will know that what is truly yours,
has found you and has stayed.
And while you are reeling in nostalgia,
the song has already changed to "Ajeeb Dastaan Hain Yeh,"
and you start humming slowly to yourself,
finally embracing the love that found you just when you were about to give up.

Searching for home

They say home is where your heart is.
But people aren't home anymore, nowadays.
They have become hotel rooms.
They check-in, stay for a while,
And leave when their vacation is over.
And you don't build homes out of hotel rooms, do you?
And maybe that is why our hearts are scattered all over the place.
And maybe that is why we desperately keep clinging on
to whatever shelter we come across.
Every time we mistake a temporary stay as our home,
we leave a piece of our heart there.
We keep hoping desperately that this time,
maybe this one last time,
we have found our homes finally.
And our hearts can finally be home probably.
But the cycle never ends. Does it?
The sun rises.
The dream breaks,
and our vacations,
just like every other time,
come to an end.
And once again,
we collect our baggage,
our shattered pieces of hopes
And desires,
shove them in the backseat
And keep driving down the bottomless abyss of hopeless dreams
with the wish of finding our home
instead of a night stay for one last time.

Disclaimer

Few things that you should know before you decide to fall in love with me!

1. I have a razor-sharp memory. I tend to remember even the most intricate details and useless things. I have never forgotten or misplaced my wallet or purse or keys or the broken pieces of my heart that had been so carelessly discarded by past lovers and friends.

2. I usually don't shut up once I start talking. They'd keep calling me the one with unlimited Talktime. However, when you need a patient ear to listen to your banters about how the colleague at your office won't stop irritating you or how you hated the morning traffic, you will know that I am always a phone call away.

3. I am usually not the one who likes bottling up her emotions and throwing them away in a far-off sea hoping for someone to make enough effort to find the message in a bottle. I am more of a person who wears her heart on her sleeve and is always ready to pour love to fill someone's cup till it spills over.

4. I usually am not great at expressing myself or my emotions. I either tend to express too much or too little. Guess, I will never know the equilibrium of emotions. Quite paradoxical for a writer, isn't it?

5. When I love, I love wholeheartedly and it sometimes gets exhausting for me and intimidating for others.

6. If anytime, someone has to impress me, all that they need to give me is a cup of good old cappuccino and a book.

So love, if you're still ready to walk into my home, you are most welcome. But if you are unsure even for a split second, I wouldn't mind if you decide to get up and leave.

A writer's den

Welcome to a writer's den
Where pain is considered to be a solace
And heartbreaks are a boon
Rather than a bane.

After all,
writing a sad poem is
a hundred times easier
than writing a love letter!

Welcome to a writer's den
Here only words can keep you sane
And all that you will find here are reels of memories and pain.

If you take a look around,
All that you will get to see is a mess.
Papers tattered. Nibs broken.
And hearts shattered.

You might ask me why don't I clean things up?
But trust me,
two heartbreaks and multiple nightmares later,
I couldn't care less.

You might not want to walk straight into the mess that I call home
And that's okay.
I understand.

After all, no one wants to mend a bruised heart that has been walked over multiple times
And be with someone
who finds poetry even in the sound of wind chimes.

Not a poem

This isn't a poem
The words don't rhyme
Neither do the sentences make sense
My poem is all over the place just like me.
It is in a disarray just like my life.

This isn't a poem.
My words won't heal you
Neither will they make you fall in love with me.
Nor will they help you find solace in your darkest nights.

This isn't a poem.
My words will not give you the adrenaline rush
or the dopamine's high to sail through life
and find happiness.

I cannot write you a poem but I can tell you that no matter how dark the tunnel looks
Or how endless the road seems,
there will always be someone to hold your hand.
There will always be someone to tell you that it gets better.

I cannot romanticize the sadness
and difficulties for you.
But all that I can give you is the assurance.
The assurance that it is going to be okay.
After all, this isn't a poem.

Writing about heartbreak

And just like that in the snap of a finger,
everything ended.
Your sweet words became a poison for me,
which I could neither swallow nor throw up.
The only memory that I have of you now is,
You receiving my call while still being in the arms of your new lover.
The only words that linger on my mind whenever your name comes up are,
"You have never been enough for me."
Maybe that's what heartbreaks are all about.
All that we tend to remember is the bitterness that our lovers leave us with as a parting gift.
And I have been no different either.
I, just like all my fellow humans only clung to the bitterness that you left me with.
But a year later,
when I am sitting with the book in my hand that you had given me on my first date,
I realize that things weren't that bad either from the start, you know.
It wasn't like from the very first day you wanted to run away from me.
It wasn't like you didn't care for me or loved me.
But the only difference is that you loved me in fragments.
You loved me only when it was convenient for you.
You loved me when you wanted a body to satiate your desires,
And an inbox to send your drunk messages to.
While I was looking for a Yin to my Yang in you,
you were searching for your past lovers in me.
Maybe all that I wanted was a friend who would stay.
But you were looking for a mirror image of yourself.
And so over time,
you did realize that I,
I can never be enough for you.

To Calcutta, With Love

I was born in a city where food comes before anything in the world.
I was born in a city where the 'aloo' in the biryani is as important as oxygen.
I was born in a city where men and women equally engage in debates over the "bhaar er cha."
I was born in a city where people deliberately decide to take the trams to cherish the age-old traditions.
I call this city my home,
my safe place.
My city knows how to make lovers unite at the Ganga ghats.
My city knows how to make poets write.
My city knows how to stand tall with its heritage intact amidst the changing times.
When the wind blows over my face while standing at the Mullick bazaar ghat,
My city tells me that it will protect me from any storm that comes over me.
My city is the one where people dance at "Ma Durga's Bhashan" with as much zeal as they cut the cake on Christmas.
My city doesn't discriminate between any festivals.
All that my city knows to do is to spread joy.
The city that I call home
Has it's dark alleys as well
In which the evil dwells
And pride swells.
But my city knows how to bring light
to end the long dark nights.
And when I look at the age-old clock at the Howrah station,
it tells me that no matter how much time passes by and how many people leave my city,
One day they will all return.
They all will return home.
It tells me that people never really leave this city.

No matter how far they go,
A part of them remains here
in the city that is so dear.

A receipe book on life

Probably life would have been easier if we had a recipe book for creating and maintaining our relationships.
Probably life would have been easier if we knew how many spoons of love and care to add and how long to simmer a relationship before it gets perfectly cooked along with a disclaimer of how anything more or anything less would ruin the highly anticipated dish.
Alas! Life doesn't come with a cookbook.
All that life gives us are the ingredients. Some way too much and some way too less.
And it is totally upon us to decide the amount of each ingredient we need to create our favorite dishes.
But not all of us will have the same favourites, you see.
And neither do all of us get the same ingredients.
We all try to make the best out of all that we are provided with.
So let everyone cook their own dishes and present before you.
At the end of the day it is up to you to decide what is your comfort food.

A letter to myself

Things that I will never be able to say out loud about myself.
1. My favourite colour is blue. But I cannot differentiate between the various shades of blue. However, I clearly remember the shades of blue the sky has on days I am sad.
2. My whole life has been one vicious cycle of hating myself and then falling in love with myself again. From hating to look at the mirror to standing in front of the mirror at least for a few minutes nowadays, I have made good progress.
3. My traumas had been a reason for me to take to writing so even though the world (read as my mom and best friends) blame those predators for ruining me to some extent, I am secretly thankful to them for making me a writer.
4. My love for food didn't arise because I loved eating. It arose because that was the only thing that provided me solace and distracted me every time someone pointed out a flaw in how I looked.
5. No matter how cool I seem, deep down I live in constant fear of losing my friends. A constant fear of them choosing someone else over me eats me from inside everytime. And that is the reason why I sometimes tend to suffocate them by showing them too much love.
6. I have always been a great talker or extrovert as they say. But never have I ever been able to construct meaningful sentences to make others understand what I want to say.
7. The sky was a shade of blue and grey combined today.

In love with the nights

I am in love with nights.
I have always been a stargazer rather than the one reveling in the sunlight.
I have always been more comfortable in darkness than in the light.
Because that was one of the very few things that connected me with my dad.
He always had an interest in the galaxies and the milky way.
And was a lover of the night rather than the day.
He'd tell me that darkness lets you be your own self.
No one's watching you and no one would reach out to you to help.
You and your scars are all by your own.
You can pull off the mask that you so carefully use as a shield in the battlefield.
At night, you are at your weakest.
All the heaviness of pretensions and the day's guilt are off your chest.
He'd also tell me that all that we have at night to keep us company is the starry night sky.
And mind you, stars don't judge.
So you can go naked revealing all your insecurities without feeling shy.
Often they'd say how lovers get lost in trance and find nights the epitome of romance.
But you see, isn't night the most scariest time to love someone?
Because nights are when everyone is in their most unadulterated versions with sharp edges and no filters and no make up.
And you know how we humans are weak at dealing with rawness.
We like everything diluted with a tinge of our own checklists.
But nights are not for fairytales, you see.
Nights are when they show you the mirror to your soul.
And if you can handle love at night, in my dad's words, you can ace in anything.
And maybe that's why I will always be in love with nights.

Love song

I was searching for a 90s love
in a generation of right swipes and Skype.
I was searching for an old school love (as you all name it)
in a generation of hookup culture and online dates.
To be honest, I had almost stopped looking.
And that's when I saw you there in the corridors talking to your friends
and laughing away with a smile so pure
that I can't put into words.
One heartbreak and a few nightmares later,
I'd found you.
But I decided to step back
and not let Dopamine's effect take over ruining me all over again.
But 3 months 5 days later,
I saw you again.
I saw you with that same smile plastered on your face
and the same innocence reflecting in your eyes.
But thank God for my sense of humour, we spoke.
You laughed at my joke
And that's how we ended up talking all night long.
Aah! Your words indeed did feel like a song.
I didn't want to trust someone once again fearing that you too would do me wrong.
But gradually,
prolonged conversations over a few cups of tea everyday made me give in to the chemical reactions in my brain.
 But now when people ask me when was the exact moment I'd start feeling something for you, I go weak in the knees and completely blank about everything.
I don't remember the exact moment when I decided to give you the key to my heart
that has been shattered in a thousand pieces
and carefully locked and hidden from the world.

I don't remember whether it was your radiating sunshine like smile
or whether it was your adorable yet quirky ways of talking.
Or wait, was it when you started feeling like home away from home?
Maybe it was when I was crying uncontrollably
and you held on to me tightly letting me know that
all that you wanted was to stay and nothing more than that.

Facing my demons

And when you are in trouble and you keep trying to get things together,
but they just keep falling apart,
That's the time when you desperately want to run away from everyone to a far off unknown land where there won't be anyone whose expectations you have to fulfil.
And when the nights are darker than they usually are,
That's the time when you wish that someone would come and switch on the light.
No. Not because you can't switch it on but because you are too tired to do so.
You have taken "Be your own hero" way too seriously.
You only kept on going through with a smiling face to live up to the image of a strong, independent person when in reality there were demons waging wars inside you.
You only hoped that someone would see through your veil and try to save you.
But hon, you forgot that your image of being a strong person was way too well portrayed to be disbelieved.
You wished that someone would tell you to stop walking through fire every day and save yourself.
But they knew that you were made of all things strong and unbreakable.
So they couldn't see that the fire was burning you little by little every day.

My mind is a battlefield

The clock says that it is 3 AM. The hour when the sane people are sleeping. But here I am, tossing in my bed constantly. No. This isn't the first time. More often than not, my habit of over thinking takes away my sleep. It is just one of those days again.
This is the hour of the ghosts and spirits, they say.
Maybe that's the reason why my demons are waging wars inside me.
Maybe that's why the ghosts of my past are haunting me incessantly.
Whole day I keep fighting against them and keep them suppressed but at this hour of the night when I am at my weakest, how can I fight them?
So I give up. I allow them to bruise me and open my age old scars once again.
I allow them to break me down once again.
But not for long because it is almost dawn and now my demons are getting weaker.
As tears of pain roll down my eyes and the sky breaks into a thousand colours, I again pick up my shield to hide my scars and put on the mask suppressing my ghosts once again.

Girls like us

Girls like us aren't meant to be loved.
Rather they don't fall for girls like us.
They don't find love in our loudness and stubbornness.
They don't find love in our overthinking and anxiety.
They don't find love in our inability to shut ourselves up.
They don't fall for girls like us.
Girls who don't pick and choose their words while expressing themselves can't be loved, can they?
Girls who value emotional connections more than facial beauty can't be loved.
Girls who sit in one corner of a bookstore quietly reading their favourite poem can't be loved.
Alas! They don't fall in love with girls like us.
Because girls like us vociferously try not to be the passive voice which they try to conveniently shut off in the name of love. Because girls like us passionately love and give their all which they can't handle and choose to run away.
Because girls like us don't make love a game that can be played whenever one is bored.

Of appearances and love

My on-point makeup, dark brown lipstick and close to perfect Kajal were what attracted you.
My elegance and grace were what made you stick around.
But when at the end of the day I removed my make-up,
and let my hair down along with my insecurities,
you found it unattractive and started to distance yourself from me little by little one day at a time.
When after a long day at work,
I let go of my grace and elegance and ranted in front of you,
you tried to turn your face away,
unwilling to accept that I too am a human and have flaws.
When the inner kid in me happily ate a bar of ice cream,
smudging it all over my face,
you were so embarrassed that you didn't even walk by my side that day.
You had only liked me for my aesthetics.
So when I removed the filters and put my unedited version in front of you,
you were intimidated and searched for ways to run away from me.
And now you ask me,
what did I see in him that I didn't see in you?
I saw in him the same 10-year-old child that resides in me who doesn't mind ice cream over my face or Biryani smell from my mouth.
I saw in him the mirror to my soul.
And this mirror not only reflected my aesthetics,
but also my rawness and embraced it completely.
I saw in him a fearless lover who loves me for who I am,
and not what I upload on my social media account to keep up with the Snapchat streaks.
Do you still want to know what I see in him?

Of dreams and fairylands

I was waiting there in the hope that you will come along
And take me away back to the fairyland
Where we will keep playing and carve our names on the sand.
Alas! the sea waves will wash them away keeping no trace just like you have removed my existence completely from your life.
Perhaps the curse of oblivion made it easier for you to move on.
Where were you when I was lost in the bottomless abyss of sadness?
Where were you when I needed you the most?
You were nowhere to be found.
You thought that my love for you was a cage in which you were trapped.
But in reality, it was my wings that were clipped and chapped.
So here I am letting you go with all my might
And freeing myself from the bondage you so precariously called love.
And now it is only your memories that keep haunting me like a ghost.
You have already gone far away from my everyday life.
But I break down into bits and pieces every night
when I recall that I will no longer be the reason for your beautiful smile.
No matter how much I cry and keep beating and battering my heart till it bleeds,
I know that you have found a better home.
I know that I don't want to come back.
And neither do you want me to save you anymore
Because my presence is no longer needed
And my absence no longer matters.

Nightmares

Do you know how nightmares look?
They are definitely not scary as described in the books.
They aren't the ones who scare you at once.
They will take their own sweet time to destroy you.
And gradually dim your shine.
That ruffled hair, shy smiles and enticing eyes will make you hypnotised.
You will forget about all those times when you have been chastised.
For a moment, that nightmare will make you feel like the luckiest person alive.
Your heart will be so full of love that
you won't even hesitate to neglect that negative vibe.
But dearest, look carefully into his eyes.
You will realise how all those promises were lies.
Nightmares never create bonds. They are there only to break all ties.
At the end of the day,
When you thought that you could finally be happy
A nightmare will come along to uplift you for a while
And then leave you to walk alone hundreds of miles.
After all, nightmares aren't the ones that scare you at once.

Paradoxes

We are a generation full of broken hearts and antidepressants and slit wrists.
We are a generation full of complexities and innumerable turns and twists.
Some of us find love in the right swipes
While some of us are old school lovers trying to find love in chance encounters.
We long to be loved
But hide behind masks of heartlessness
And push everyone away.
And often at night when the world is silent
And we no longer need to pretend,
We put down our masks and dream of forevers and fairy tales
And secretly pray for our wishes to come true.

We long to hold someone's hands and dance and sway in the rain
But we are too worried about missing the last train.
We love to be strong
And be alone
But once in a while
When we breakdown
And cry our hearts out in the corner of our rooms,
We secretly wish for someone to send us a loving message.
We can't mix and match our feelings and emotions with our words as easily as we can match our accessories with our clothes.
While we are trying to find the figures of speech that suit our poems and verses the best,
We ourselves are full of paradoxes and ironies, you see.

Firsts

You will always be my first late-night phone call,
My first sent love letter
And my first kiss.
Probably you will wake up one fine day and decide you can't do this anymore.
Or probably I will get so tired of your selfless love that I will decide to walk away.
But those few firsts will always be mine.
You will always be my home.
My safe place to hide from the world's cruelties.
Probably a storm might come and break down my home.
But you will always be the strength I need to build it up again.
You will always be the one I would want to watch the stars under the Parisian sky.
And you will always be the one I would want to run back to.

Building blocks

At 4,
My mother taught me how to use building blocks to learn alphabets.
At 8,
My grandmother told me that women need to be constructed piece by piece.
Similar to Lego sets, isn't it?
Purity, silence, composure and tolerance are the building blocks of being a perfect woman,
She said,
Oh! And she also added that one block here or there can instantly remove me from the position of a perfect daughter, sister, wife et cetera.
At 13,
Aunties in my neighbourhood told me that smoking and drinking can break down my character
which has been so carefully built by my family
using society's instruction manuals.
At 16,
The boy I fell in love with told me
 I couldn't be loved because I was loud
and stubborn
and didn't fit into the description of girls he has learnt so far.
But at 21, finally
I started to deconstruct myself and throw away the building blocks stuck in my foundation.
I started to build myself by unlearning the alphabets and words fed by society
And probably that day I started to get my vocabulary correct.

Stay

Stay a little longer.
For I need you to inscribe poetry on my skin.
For I need you to heal my wounds using your figures of speech.
Stay. A little longer.
For I wish to see a few more sunsets with you.
For I wish to walk along the beaches wearing my favourite sunflower yellow dress holding your hands.
Stay a little longer.
For I need you to know how effortlessly you have undone my fears.
Stay! A little longer.
For people have only walked away from my life and I have forgotten how it feels when someone holds on.
Stay a little longer.
For I need to pour out all my love that I hold for you.
For I need to make love to you on those freshly ironed white bedsheets like there's no tomorrow.
Stay. A little longer.
For I need your body to stay intertwined with mine
till the end of the world.

Parallel universe

Let us assume, it was a beautiful night.
Let us assume, you and I didn't part that night.
Let us assume that night wasn't our last one together.
Let us assume, you weren't the one who made all the promises but in the end left our home, abruptly banging the door behind you.
My Love, let us assume that you and I will again meet to complete our unfinished poems and the painting on your canvas.
Let us assume that the probability of you and me staying together is one.
And lastly, you won't love anyone else as much as you loved me.

Home

Honey, you were never the one to settle.
Hell, you were never the one to create a permanent shelter out of another human being either.
So tell me, what made you create a home out of him?
Tell me, what made you hand over your jagged and wounded heart
in spite of knowing that he too could throw it away in the blink of an eye?
Was it your increasing emptiness in your life?
Or was it the need to finally lie down and rest knowing that you are not alone in this war anymore?
Probably it was the forehead kiss on a drunken night.
Probably it was the wiping off your face when you,
like a child,
ecstatically licked off the last remnants of the ice cream in the container.
Or maybe it was the messages he left for you when you were crying yourself to sleep with absolutely no willingness to go through yet another battle.
Or do I say it was all those things he did for you that you deserved but no one else could ever give you?

Someone like you

They'd warn me to not fall for the hazel eyes, the crooked smiles, the sweet words.
They'd warn me that people like you are too good to be true.
They'd say that someone like you who remembers the tiniest details like how I like my ice cream, a little melted with excess choco chips, my favourite line from a book, or my hatred for late replies
Is an error 404: not to be found.
They'd say that men like you could only be a character straight outta Cecelia Ahern's novels.
They'd call me naive, stupid to have thought that someone like you could exist in reality.
They'd mock me to believe in the existence of fairytales and knights in shining armour.
Oh! Honey, they'd warn me to stop day dreaming
And stay away from a fictional build up of you.
But they haven't known you the way I have.
They haven't thrown open the gates of their hearts for anyone in spite of being broken the way you have.
So here I am in the middle of the night talking to you
and thinking how they were all stupid to have thought that
all of this is only an impossible dream
that I hold close to my heart.
Here I am thinking how incredibly lucky I am to have found someone like you.

Indomitable

She is a girl of indomitable spirits
With a heart of gold.
She knows what to do
And what not to.
She never needs to be told.

Her enigmatic beauty is way beyond
the predefined notions of prettiness.
Her elegance and grace
Has no fallacy's trace.

Her bright smile
Can give anyone the courage
To go an extra mile.

She loves to dance in the rain
And laugh and keep chirping like a bird.
She is a girl full of happiness and mirth.
And surely nowadays, such people are a dearth.

But then again, she knows how to stand up against the wrong
And has the courage to face what
comes along.
She has been doing this lifelong
And it keeps on making her strong.
She is a girl
Who is as precious as a pearl
And who knows her dreams
Are for real.

Opposites

You have been the one who has been loved by everyone under all circumstances.
And it was no exception for me either.
Your puns and anecdotes were all that it took for me to start falling for you.
But I, I am the rusted soul that isn't needed in this generation.
I am not the one accepted or loved by most.
I have been the one who has always felt out of place even in a room full of acquaintances.
I have been the boring one who never really had much to offer.
I have been the one with whom people really don't fall in love.
And you have been no exception either.
They say that feelings can't be forced.
But they also force me to get over you.
Quite a paradox, isn't it?
Believe me, I'd try to find flaws in you that would make me hate and curse and rip you apart
And force me to push you into oblivion.
But the more I tried to push you away, the deeper I fell into the bottomless abyss called love.
It has been a few days
Or rather 8 months 12 days and 5 hours since you have last spoken to me.
You remember me, don't you?
Or am I just another contact on your list who doesn't matter to you anymore?
I wonder how you have been.
I wonder whether I even crossed your mind once.
I know you don't have time to spare a thought about my existence.
I know you have better things to keep your mind preoccupied with.
After all, you have always been the one who never found it necessary to remember unnecessary things like

my favourite colour,
the lyrics of my favourite song,
my crooked smile
And now my existence.
And I like a fool have diligently memorised even the tiniest details related to you
like the colour of the button of the shirt you wore on our first date,
your favourite ice cream flavour,
And now your absence in my life.

Down the memory lane

Come with me for a walk, will you?
Let us walk through those streets surrounded by book stores once again.
Hand in hand we will walk along fighting over our favourite authors and their books
And not caring about people giving us weird looks.

How have you been lately?
I wonder about you often when I pass by that favourite bookshop of yours.
My heart still craves for those alluring eyes of yours while you scan through the shelves.
Alas! Some wounds have no cures.

I still pick up that book of poems which you absolutely loved
and smile at the thought of how we used to fight over who was better. Dante or Milton?

After you left, I never could find that same warmth in those bookstores.
It seemed as if everything was a bore.

I did meet many people along but none could ignite in me that spark which you had done and left a mark.

Days and months have passed by but my thoughts have still remained stagnant.
What exactly did life mean?
I don't know.
Nothing made sense since the 1st of April.
Yes. That was the day you had gone away.
Far far away from all these bookstores and me.
And you took away along with you my life's key.

Tonight

Tonight let us keep aside everything and talk about our fears.
Tell me about your biggest fears and I will share with you the stories that scared me the most.
Tell me whether it is the monsters under your bed that make you horrified or the imaginary ghosts in your dreams that make you sweat in your sleep?
Tonight let us put our guard down and embrace each other's fears and inhibitions.
For a change, let us stop pretending and let out all that we have bottled up inside us.
What takes away your sleep?
Is it the fear of something unknown or the fear of being broken by the known?
I will tell you what makes me sad now and then and you too will let out what is killing you inside.
Let us make love to each other tonight not through our bodies but through our words.
I know that you have trusted someone else before with your weaknesses and have been hurt. But dearest, I will make sure that you don't have to feel insecure about your flaws and imperfections anymore.
I won't promise to take away your fears.
Instead, I assure you to help you in all ways possible to get over even the most dreadful memory of your life.
Oh love! Don't you worry anymore because tonight will be the night when I will listen to all that you have to say and kiss away all your inhibitions.
I will take care of your bruises and nurse them till they finally get healed.
 I have nothing more to give you my love.
All that I have is love, care and patience.
And tonight, I want to give all that away to you.
All that I ask from you is just hold on and sit by my side at least for this night.
So, what are you waiting for, love?

Train of thoughts

Whenever I look around,
I see lovers walking hand in hand lost in their
own wonderland.
Fake or real, I know not.
Whenever I look around,
I see young boys and girls looking at their phones,
probably blushing too on receiving certain text messages.
Whenever I look around,
I see chatty people and happy faces and crying infants.
I see people expressing emotions and mingling with the crowd and sometimes getting lost in it too.
But whenever I look around,
I don't find myself fitting into any category.
I feel I am the only one who can't be tracked down in the map of emotions.
I, I feel out of place.
I either end up expressing too much or too little.
Or rather most of the time, I end up wrapping my emotions with overdoses of profanity.
And nowadays mostly at nights,
When the world's all asleep and there's only stillness,
I find myself wondering about why I am the one who is always left behind by people or walked over.
But you will be surprised to know that I no longer feel amazed or betrayed.
My tears can no longer be traced.
And it is because I have been graced with the knowledge that no one likes to handle a wreck
amidst all the calmness.

Everytime

Everytime I look at the clouds
they seem to create trails that would lead me to you.
Everytime the leaves rustle and the birds sing,
their sounds resemble your voice whispering sweet nothings into my ears.
And everytime the cool summer breeze touch my burning skin,
They resemble your hands digging into the crests and valleys of my body and caressing me while taking me to the zenith of pleasure.
And when everytime someone offers to buy me a drink at the bar by the street where you have walked me down a thousand times,
I never forget to order your favourite drink for myself.
Oh! And how can I ever forget that
Everytime when I am in the bookstore ,
I end up picking Neruda or Rumi wishing you'd read them aloud to me one day.
And everytime when someone plays the medleys of old hindi songs
Or strikes the chords of "You look wonderful tonight"
I can't help but recall your voice singing them as lullabies to me every night.
And when someone asks me
about my favourite song,
I always end up humming the ones
you have sung for me so far.
And even though winters make me want to give up my life for it,
Everytime it rains, I step out and let those tiny droplets make love to my skin because you say that monsoons are your favourite.
And how can I not allow your favourite season of monsoon to drench me in its love potion everytime I start missing you!
I rehearse and imagine and reimagine how I would be the first one to run and hug you
and kiss you till my lips hurt
the next time I see you,

Not in my dreams
But the time when I can touch and feel you with my frail fingers.
But Everytime I see you standing in front of me,
I go weak in the knees
and all my thoughts which I had so carefully sorted in separate folders of my mind
And checked and rechecked them for a millionth time
get messed up again.
All those scenes that I had run
and rerun in my head vanish into thin air
leaving me clueless as to what in you makes me so unmindful everytime I see you.

You & I

I thought I would write a poem for you,
I ended up writing hardly a line or two.
I thought I would tell you all that I wanted to,
I ended up only saying I love you.
I probably know hardly anything about romance.
But one thing I did really want to have with you is a rain dance.
Getting drunk and singing my heart out is not something I think I would do.
But I don't mind if it's with you.
I know that reading poetry alone is something that only I have always loved to do.
But I wish I could read them with you too.
You know how I can't shut up once I start talking.
But I run out of words whenever my friends take your name and keep mocking.
It's not because I have nothing to say.
It's because if they knew about you, most likely they too would fall in love with you.
And that's probably the last thing I would want
For you are mine to keep and I can't share.
 I just can't.

Bottled up

You ask me why I always shut myself up when I feel sad.
The last time I opened up and spoke my heart out,
Someone told me not to nag over petty issues because the world had better things to worry about.

Now you know why don't I open up anymore?
I keep on bottling things inside even if I want to cry out vehemently from my heart's core.
Because the last time I opened up
Someone told me that I was an attention seeker.

You ask me why can't I rely upon people and lay my weaknesses open sometimes.
The last time I kept my scars bare, Someone got scared of my reality and left me alone in the middle of nowhere.

You ask me why I don't depend on people sometimes and always take everything on me.
The last time I tried to look for a hand to hold,
Someone told me that I was clingy.

And do you have to ask me why I have become so cranky and irritated?
The last time I was angry and wanted comfort,
Someone told me that I was always whining.

And you still think that I suppress myself for no reason?

Beauty?

You ask me why do I laugh a little less these days or turn away my face while smiling.
Well, last time when I laughed heartily, someone told me that my gums were visible and it made me look ugly.
I laughed it away showing how light a matter it was.
But for the next three days, I cried myself to sleep and didn't come out of my house.
I am not the one to cry in front of people, you see.
You ask me why I often become so conscious in front of the camera.
The last time I was clicking a selfie, someone told me that I didn't look good enough.
And since then I can't face the mirror without taking this thought out of my mind.
You ask me why I always try to tie my hair tightly into a bun.
Because the last time I let it loose, someone just said that my hair is what makes me the ugliest.
And the last time, the last time I fell in love,
someone just said that they deserved someone prettier than me.
Now you know why I push people away and have cooped myself up.

Not your cup of tea

I might not be the shiny and decked up pretty girl whom everyone likes at one go.
I might not be the person who can be a trophy girlfriend.
But I can definitely be a person who can immensely love someone if she decides to.
I can shower you with love and care to such an extent that it will remove all your pain
And I can assure that will definitely be your gain.
I can give my best to make one happy.
But I won't be the person who will be so easy to deal with.
I definitely am not the person one dreams of
But I can be the person who will support you to fulfil all your dreams.
I am a person with scars on my skin and soul.
I am the one whose days and nights often remain as dark as coal.
But remember just like diamonds come out of coal,
I can shine too if you can set me free and not chain me down in the name of love
Because that will only make my soul drown in the bottomless abyss of sadness and frown.
But if you can brush aside my bruises,
You will get a person who will break down all her barriers to love you
But will never ever make you feel possessed.
Be it for a day or forever,
I am the person who will make you feel special in all possible ways.
If you think I am insane enough for you to handle me,
You are free to walk away
But I will still remain the person who knows to play a song even with broken strings.
All you have to do is love me and place your trust in me.
And the rest will be taken care of. You will surely lead your life in happiness and glee.

But I am not an easy person to be with.
I will be the most vulnerable soul and at times the strongest of all.
But if you can withstand me in every situation then only you can be a part of my rise and fall.
You might be scared to gulp down the stark reality about myself
And might not have the courage to stand by me
But I don't blame you for this.
Not all can take a risk of keeping a girl who isn't even sure what will be the next thing about her that will be unfurled.
Take me as you want or leave me the way I am and if latter is the option you choose then

Invincible

She is a woman of invincible spirit.
Her eyes narrate stories.
Her lips carve out the words she wants to speak
and not the ones pasted on her face by the dear society.
Her face shines as bright as a pearl and she knows how to make her dreams real.
She can be as calm as the ocean
But can also bring out the fire in her whenever required.
She can give away her life for the ones
she cares about
But she can also take away everything from the ones who don't deserve it.
Her will power and strength is what keeps her going.
The way she looks at life
And the way she carries herself is the reason why people respect her.
You love her
And she will embrace you with all her heart. But once you trigger her,
You will get to see what storms look like.
She is a woman.
A woman of strength and will.
She can rock the cradle
And rule the world at the same time.

Our first date

A table for two by the windows that you found aesthetic.
Hours of judging people together.
Endless conversations.
And lots of common interests shared.
From favourite books to favourite ice cream flavours,
We exchanged a lot.
But after 2 hours,
When you were leaving
Something sank inside me.
And I realised that this was the first time
I wanted someone to stay a little longer.
No. I didn't tell you to wait back
Or spend some more time
Because the self-dependant obsessed girl in me didn't want to fall back on someone.
But some things aren't really in our control, are they?
And although I didn't tell you anything,
I fervently kept praying for you to not leave.

One last time

If you see me breaking down someday,
don't you turn back and bother to pick up my broken pieces.
Don't bother to come running to me with those false hugs and kisses.
If you see me someday lost in the bottomless abyss of tears and me giving into my fears,
don't come running to me to put my pieces together again.
I say this because I have put up with things for far too long.
Even the guitar's broken strings have given up on playing my favourite song.
Even the bokeh lights have now become dim.
Everything in my life has started to give up.
How do you expect me to hold back anymore?
How long do you expect me to hide all the scars and fly high and soar?
How long?
Can you tell me?
I have given up and so has my soul.
I have lost the battle.
I couldn't get through this time anymore.
I couldn't save myself anymore.
Don't you worry, I will be alright.
I might not be able to fight but I will not bother you anymore.
I will survive and stay alive even if I can't live my life.
I have fought through every strife and here I give up finally.
I am sorry if this might make you bored.
I write to you out of despair.
I write to you for one last time before I give up.

Lights out

Last night the light in my room was flickering constantly
And I didn't make an effort to get up and switch it off.
I didn't make an effort to end those little rays of hope
And call darkness upon me.
No. I don't have that strength.
I don't have the capacity to completely end everything with a snap of my fingers.
I let things blink and flicker as much as they want instead of completely dying out
And leaving me alone
Because as a child I had always been afraid of being left out.
I had always been afraid of the world being oblivious to my presence.
And I had always felt that Oblivion is the most lethal weapon that mankind has been cursed with.
And I, I am scared of it.
I am scared that I will not be visible enough to make a place in this world
Or to mark my own territory.
I fear that there will always be people to pull me down
And push me down the black hole of forgetfulness.
So I cling on to the slightest ray of light in the hope that I can let people know that I still exist in the room.
I cling on to the last bits and pieces of my strength to let everyone know
That I still am alive
And that I will not let myself fizzle out so soon like the shooting star upon which you wished to forget me.

Departures

I have seen people crying over goodbyes and departures.
I have seen people being sad over not being able to meet their friends and lovers for months together.
But for me, it was different,
You know.
Goodbyes never really hurt me,
You see.
I never really missed people or cried when they left the city. "Oh! What a pity." They used to say that to me.
I have seen acquaintances and friends and lovers and family leaving, sometimes the city
And sometimes my life.
But then nothing ever left a mark to last enough for me to crave for them.
But life laughed at me when I bumped into you.
Goodbyes meant nothing until it was you whom I had to bid farewell.
Departures too were meaningless for me until it was you in whose heart I wanted to dwell.
Now I know what it means to stand at airports and wait keenly for your loved ones.
Now I know what it takes to stay far from them and wait for those few days when you get to meet them.
And for the first time,
I too felt the pain of hugging someone and bidding farewell.
I too didn't want to let you go
For I wanted to hold on to you
As long as I could.

Seasons

My love for you isn't seasonal
It changes its intensity with time but it never withers away like the leaves during fall.
Neither does it become as vibrant as the budding flower during the spring for the world to acknowledge its existence.
My love for you might take a backseat when I am all tensed up
And drained out like the tired old man during summers.
But it won't fail to keep you warm
like a cup of hot chocolate on a cold, chilly winter day.
My love for you isn't as colourful and attractive as the trees before the season of fall.
But it is all embracing and comforting like a glass of cold water on a summery day.
My love for you isn't as photogenic as the summer beaches or raindrops dripping down the window shields.
But it surely is as memorable as the first shower of rain after the hot and exhausting summers.
Lastly, I hope that your love for me isn't seasonal either.

Writers and their magic

Often, you appreciate my poetry.
You tell me how I articulate words with great eloquence.
You tell me how magically I express the deepest and unspoken feelings of many in general through the verses and stanzas that I create.
But have you ever tried to realise how those words come to me so naturally?
They say that writers write what they feel most of the times,
and I am no exception either.
You tell me how perfectly I express the loneliness
that lies within us hiding behind the facade of a smiling face.
That's exactly what I do too.
Masquearading my feelings with the words that I write.
Writers do not always write for validation.
Often, they resort to pen and paper to let their feelings out
which they cannot express verbally in the fear of being clingy
or an attention seeker.
They aren't really good with their verbal communication.
Mostly writers are the ones who give credit to their imaginary thoughts
when asked about their writings.
But in reality it is their suppressed emotions
and their hopes
and desires that give wings to their writings.
Writers aren't as brave as their writings might make you think them to be.
On the contrary, they are the ones who use their writings as an escapade
to run far away from their heartbreaks,
and losses.
They are the ones who wrap their pain with verses,
and phrases,
and paragraphs,
and present before you as those literary pieces you admire so much.

Ruins

I have a weird fetish for ruined and broken buildings.
I have a deep rooted attachment to age old streets and lanes.
Probably because I love history a lot.
Or maybe I can connect them to my own broken pieces.
I marvel at how beautifully they are holding themselves with the last remaining strength.
I wonder whether I too have the same will to keep moving in the hope that others find beauty in the scattered and ruined pieces of my heart just like they find beauty in the last remnants of old monuments.
I wonder whether anyone wishes to capture and showcase the remnants of my love the way they snapchat and instagram the pictures of the broken and artistic buildings and proudly show it to the world boosting their photography skills.
Do people marvel on hearing my stories the way the are in awe of the stories of those ruins?
Or do I just bore them and all that they see is emptiness?
And on days when these historic places and old ruins become a writer's muse, I wonder if I ever can be in a writer's thoughts or on a painter's canvas.

Missing

We don't get to choose when we will miss someone.
We don't get to decide when their absence suddenly engulfs us in an unknown void.
It might just be a random visit to their favourite hangout spot
or something as simple as eating the flavour of ice cream that they love the most.
But if you ask me,
I would hardly be able to mark those random fleeting moments when I wish for you to be here.
I miss you when I am sitting in the desolate metro stations alone.
I miss you when I miss trains
and think about how we ran
from one platform to another to board the train once when you were in the city
and I was happy after a long time.
I would be lying if I say I miss you all the time.
But I would also be lying if I act uber cool
And say that I don't really miss you at all.
But whenever these sudden pangs of sadness hits me
And whenever I visit a bookstore or see something aesthetic
and get reminded of you,
the only thing that keeps me going is that someday this distance and sudden rush of tears will be worth it.
And that day when I will look back at these moments,
I will be grateful that I didn't give up.

Forever?

And sometimes no matter how hard you try to keep drilling it into your mind that "Forever is a lie"
and nothing really stays,
it still lingers at the back of your mind that maybe forever exists.
You still wish to believe in fairy tales like you once did.
No matter how hard you try to rationalise that it is okay for people to leave and things to fall apart,
sometimes you want to give up on your logic,
and embrace the stupid human heart's illogical
and irrational hopes
and expectations.
Some days even the most practical people dream
and hope
and cry
and wish that at least once their practicality fails and their heart wins.
And more often than not you think that suppressing your own idealistic dreams
and wishes can make you feel that you belong to the mass
but deep down you still try to make yourself believe that what you hope for is true
and you can make people stay.

Love in the times of pandemic

We fell in love at a strange time, love.
We fell in love when the world was at war.
We fell in love when people were fighting their fears, anxieties,
And their constant need to keep their loved ones safe.
I, for one, was never looking for someone to embrace me,
And whisper into my ears that everything will be okay when my anxieties act up
Or when I panic about being away from my family amidst the crisis.
And you too were not looking for someone to keep you up at night with banters
while you watch your football games.
And maybe,
That is why I believe that we get what we want when we are not looking for it at all.
And maybe,
that is why I believe that we can't decide days, timings, or occasions to fall in love
Because love happens when we are not ready for it.
Love happens when we are on the edge almost ready to give up on the idea that love exists.

Confessions

Tell me the first time you said "I like you" to me, it felt a little different this time.

Tell me the first time you said you loved me, you shed a tear because I made you feel a sweet sixteen kind of love.

Tell me the first time you held my hand, you felt a jolt of current in your body like the thunder struck clouds making love to the city skies.

Tell me the first time you kissed me, your fingers traced a cyclone on my back while you meticulously marked your territory on my neck.

Tell me the first time we laughed together in the front seat of your car, the barren earth burst with hope and life.

Tell me the first time we made love to each other, you felt loved and safe and cared for because I, for one, felt that way.

Tell me these firsts were serendipity, because I had stopped believing in miracles before our universes collided.

About the Author

Ishita Bagchi

"If I do not speak in a language that can be understood there is little chance for a dialogue."

~Bell Hooks

This is a quote that inspires Ishita and her need to express herself through her writings. Ishita is a public policy consultant by profession and an avid reader and a writer by passion. She has a keen interest in economics and literature. She believes that words and ideas can change the world and there is no greater weapon than words. She started writing only to express herself but she never realised when this hobby of hers turned into a passion that kept her up at nights for hours.

Twitter: @ishitabagchi98

Instagram: @the_whimsical_poetess

www.ingramcontent.com/pod-product-compliance
Lightning Source LLC
LaVergne TN
LVHW041222080526
838199LV00082B/1873